BETTER BROCHURES, CATALOGS AND MAILING PIECES

By Jane Maas

ST. MART

Copyright © 1981 by Jane Maas
For information, write: St. Martin's Press,
175 Fifth Avenue, New York, N.Y. 10010
Manufactured in the United States of America

Library of Congress Cataloging in Publication Date

Maas, Jane.
Better brochures, catalogs, and mailing pieces.

1. Sales letters.   I. Title.
HF5730.M29   658.8′2   80-27770
ISBN 0-312-07730-0
ISBN 0-312-07731-9 (pbk.)

10 9 8 7 6

Jacket and book design by Tony Esposito

For Michael

Contents

Introduction

This book was written to fill a specific need. As part of my work on the "I Love New York" tourism program, I gave a series of seminars to groups all over New York State. The audiences were made up of people who run hotels and motels, museums, theme parks, wineries, ski centers, historic sites, and other attractions.

My discussion of print and radio advertising received polite attention. When I turned to the subject of brochures, however, suddenly pads and pencils appeared, and my audience came alive. Obviously, not everyone has a budget for advertising, but almost every business produces some type of promotional material, whether it is one simple flier or many elaborate booklets. Yet, to my knowledge, no creative guidelines had ever been set down. For the first time, then, they are presented here.

Some brochures are clearly more effective than others, in attracting attention, inviting readership, and most important of all, making the sale. The rules and examples included in the following pages simply point out what usually works and suggests some pitfalls to avoid.

Chapter Two gives you basic guidelines that apply to any brochure. Although some chapters are specifically devoted to special types of literature, I believe the hotelier will profit from reading the chapter on tourism, the college promotion director from that on hotels.

Once you understand the rules, you will be able to follow the most important one of all: break any rule for a good reason.

The introduction above was written in 1980. Since that time, audiences interested in creating better brochures have invited me to Japan and Africa, to the Rockies and the Adirondacks—and dozens of places in between.

Sales promotion has become more important than ever. No wonder so many advertising agencies, including my own, have increasingly set up separate divisions devoted to its creation.

No question but brochures are getting better. Onward!

Jane Maas
New York, 1984

SEE NEW YORK
YOUR WAY.

I Love New York at Night Show Tours
offer you an unlimited choice
for the kind of vacation experience
you'll never forget.

FAMOUS RADIO CITY MUSIC HALL ROCKETTES

Something different each night. A variety of package tours offering you an unequalled opportunity to sample the fabulous entertainment wares New York has to offer. Hotels, restaurants, Broadway's hottest hit shows are yours for the asking. So are music and ballet at

Lincoln Center, supper at Sardi's or the Chateau Madrid, dancing at the Rainbow Room on top of Rockefeller Center. Whatever kind of tour you choose, you'll get a terrific combination of shows, restaurants and other entertainment features.

Your brochure must reflect the positioning of your product. Here, New York City sells its nightlife.

CHAPTER I

The Most Important Decision: Positioning and Strategy

"I Love New York Broadway Show Tours," declares the cover of a New York State Department of Commerce brochure. The illustration is a dazzling theater marquee. Inside, the pages are splashed with colorful photos of Broadway shows. Dozens of tour packages are suggested, most including first-class hotels and orchestra seats to hit plays. The mood of the piece is sophisticated; the copy is breezy.

This successful brochure promoting New York City vacations did not just "happen." It was based on a positioning and strategy which had been agreed upon long before a word of copy was written. They determined what was said in the brochure, to whom, and how.

New York City was positioned as a uniquely exciting place to visit, because of its glamour and nightlife, especially Broadway. This decision was based on a market research study that indicated Broadway theater is the city's single most appealing attraction—head and shoulders above any other. The positioning, of course, determined the overall execution of the brochure.

The next step was a strategy statement that

included these five key points:

1. Objective—to convince consumers to visit New York City instead of other vacation destinations, especially for weekend holidays. (Note that this is a *competitive* objective. Good strategies identify the opposition.)

2. Target audience—people interested in nightlife, especially the theater. The research also pointed out that the best potential city visitors tend to be more affluent, urban and better educated than the norm. These factors dictated the brochure's emphasis on upscale packages, as well as its sophisticated style.

3. Consumer benefit—only New York City offers the excitement of Broadway. This benefit was highlighted on every page, with photographs of scenes and stars.

4. Support—package tours make a visit to New York City economical and easy. The offer of packages, including theater and meals, was designed to allay concerns about vacation costs noted in the research.

5. Tone and manner—the "personality" of the brochure is exciting, dramatic and sophisticated, like the product it is selling.

This "I Love New York" brochure did its part in the most successful tourism campaign in the United States. To a large degree, its success is due to effective positioning.

Too many brochures and catalogs today look and sound just like every other one on the subject. Too many are created without planning, without thought for the long-term impact. So the first decision you must make is also your most important: what is your positioning? Then, what is the strategy? The effectiveness of your literature depends more on this decision than on any other.

Positioning, quite simply, is placing your product or service a certain way in the consumer's mind. Do you want your hotel to stand for the utmost in modern efficiency, or for old-world charm? Is your theme park the most educational, or the scariest? Once you have decided on the positioning, you need a strategy to get you there.

Put the strategy in writing, and get agreement in advance from everyone who will be involved in the creation or approval of the brochure. A good strategy always includes the five points listed above.

1. Objective—what do you want your brochure to accomplish? For example, do you want to convince *more* customers to visit your destination? Or persuade the same customer to come more often? Or stay longer?

2. Target audience—who is your consumer? You cannot talk to everyone. Attempting to do so simply wastes money.

3. Consumer benefit—why should the consumer buy your product, visit your attraction or enroll at your college? There can be only *one* key consumer benefit. Determine which has the most importance to your particular audience.

4. Support—a reason to believe that benefit. Brochure readers are on the alert for "over-promise" and puffery. A reason to believe the message adds credibility to your story.

5. Tone and manner—the "personality" of your product or service. For many of the areas discussed in this book—tourism destinations, hotels, attractions, colleges—this brand image may well be the very thing you are selling. It is often the only element that sets you apart from your competition. Yet few brochures project a distinctive personality.

Nine Ways to a Better Strategy

Points to consider as you decide on the strategy that is best for the product you are selling.

1. Set yourself apart from the pack.

Look for a niche your competition is not filling. Cut away from the herd, and your brochure will stand out on the rack.

> *The United States Virgin Islands highlighted a unique advantage over other island vacation spots. During a period of unrest in the Caribbean, their brochures emphasized the fact that they were friendly, safe territories of the United States.*

2. Preempt the truth.

Of course, you must tell the truth. However, suppose that your hotel and that of the competitor down the street both face a lovely lake. You put a photograph of the lake on the front of your brochure with copy that states, "The lake is just a minute away." Your competitor does not mention the lake in his brochure. So you have preempted the truth.

*A number of New York City hotels face
Central Park. However, the Barbizon Plaza
has set itself apart as the hotel "with the
park at our own front door." The brochure
cover shows the hotel literally rising from
the trees, and cover copy states it is
"directly on Central Park."*

3. Study your competition.

Spread all the competitive brochures you
can find on a table. Ask yourself what strategy
each is following; what consumer benefit each
makes. Is there an obvious vacancy you can fill?
Are they saying something you can say better, or
support more believably?

4. Understand your target audience.

It isn't necessary to spend thousands of
dollars on sophisticated research. *Do* earmark
one item in your budget for some type of study.
Find out who your consumers are, what your
chief appeal is, and both positive and negative
perceptions. What attitudes set your potential
consumer apart from others?

*The Six Flags theme parks know that their
best customers are families with children
who want an economical holiday.
Brochures always depict parents and
children enjoying themselves together. Copy
mentions family-oriented benefits, such as
picnic grounds and child-care facilities, and
suggests inexpensive motels and camp sites
nearby.*

13

5. Make your benefit meaningful.

If the brochure is to do its job, the benefit offered must be important to the consumer. As helpful as it is to set yourself apart from competition, it is senseless to advertise anything the consumer does not care about.

Amtrak could have highlighted comfort, economy, safety or other benefits. However, its brochure focused on a meaningful benefit that airlines cannot deliver: "The close-up way to see the U.S.A."

6. Make your benefit believable.

Convince the consumer with a reason to believe what you say. Give facts, show photographs, use testimonials for authenticity or cite research you have conducted. You must support the benefit.

Queen Elizabeth 2 is positioned as "the greatest ship in the world." The brochure supports this statement with dozens of facts and photographs on her size, speed, accommodations and cuisine.

7. Be single-minded.

Your brochure cannot be all things to all people, or it ends up being neuter. The great advertising man David Ogilvy has said: "The capon never rules the roost."

The Western Reserve Historical Society in Cleveland is made up of seven different museums. Their one-page flier zeroed in on the single most popular area: Indians.

8. Develop a product personality.

Most products and services shamble through life without a personality. If you are lucky enough to have one, cherish it in every piece of literature you do. Do not allow any fad, no matter how tempting, to change your brand image.

> *Pinehurst, the famous North Carolina resort, is proud of its eighty-year-old heritage. The brand image projected in its literature is civilized and gentle—a portrait of the way life used to be.*

9. Stick with your strategy.

It should not be changed lightly. If you have arrived at a strategy with thought, spend more thought—and work—before you discard it. You can change the appearance and copy of your brochure as often as you wish, but its basic nature should not change from year to year.

Before you review the copy and layout of your next brochure, review the strategy. Ask yourself if the brochure is on strategy and is consistent with your brand personality. If it is not, go back to the drawing board.

A good strategy, like a good map, gets you where you want to be—faster and easier. Follow the strategy, and your brochure will be successful in doing its only real job: making the consumer take action.

Look for story-telling visuals that involve the reader and help state your benefit.

CHAPTER II

Fifteen Basic Rules for Better Brochures

Where do you begin in creating an effective brochure? Fully 50 percent of your effort should be directed toward the *cover*. It must telegraph your basic message and your personality; grab the reader and make him want to open the pages. (The first and most important rule about brochures, below, concerns the cover.)

You can forget everything else you read in this book—except this chapter—and still be ahead of the game. Follow these fifteen basic principles, and you will have a better brochure.

1. Put your selling message on the cover.

This is the most important rule of all and, curiously, one that is little followed. The cover of a brochure works like the headline of a print advertisement. *Four out of five people never get beyond it!* If you depend on the inside pages to make the sale, you are wasting 80 percent of your money.

Too many brochures use an attractive photograph on the cover, without any identification at all, not even the name of the product. These "blind" covers tell the reader nothing; they give him no incentive to turn the page.

Use the cover to state your position or promise a meaningful benefit to the consumer.

> *Chicago's Arlington Park Towers proclaims on the cover that it is: "The only hotel in the world with its own racetrack and golf course."*

At the very least, make sure the cover tells the reader who you are, where you are and what you offer.

> *The historic town of Smithville, New Jersey, states it has: "Three wonderful restaurants. Over two dozen fascinating shops. And a living, working Early American town." The cover tells the whole story.*

2. Insist on a "family resemblance" with your advertising.

If you do advertise, then your brochure must march to the same drummer. Follow the same strategy, expand on the campaign theme, use the familiar graphics and logo. Take advantage of the synergism that occurs when the brochure restates the advertising theme.

> *The advertising theme for The Bahama Islands has long been the promise that "It's better in The Bahamas." Every brochure carries the same message on the cover.*

Consistency makes every dollar work harder.

3. Use a single illustration on the cover.

Research suggests that one large illustration is more effective than several small ones. Illustrations with story appeal that involve the reader add impact. So do bright colors.

> *The covers of Olson's Tours literature "pop out" of travel agents' racks with their use of large, storytelling illustrations, always in vivid colors.*

4. Select pictures that tell a story.

The right cover photograph can often express your positioning better than words. A storytelling photo will stop the reader and make him ask: "What's going on here?"

> *A casual young woman in sneakers lounges in an elegant, throne-like chair. This juxtaposition sums up the positioning of San Diego's Little America Westgate Hotel: "European elegance and the California style."*

5. Always put captions under photographs.

Readership of captions is almost double that of body copy. Next to the cover, captions are the best-read element of any brochure. Yet not more than one out of five brochures bothers to caption photographs. A pity.

> *The State of Oregon uses long, informative captions that virtually serve as the text of the piece. A photo of Crater Lake, for instance, is captioned: "Incredibly blue Crater Lake, 57 miles north of Klamath Falls, is the center of its own national park. The 1,932-foot-deep lake is set in a crater formed by the collapse of a prehistoric volcano. A 35-*

*mile rim drive offers varied views of the
lake and Wizard and Phantom Ship islands.
Crater Lake Park has a lodge, cottages and
camping accommodations."*

Captions that give the reader lots of information
work harder than short, bland ones. How much
less effective the caption above would have been
if it stopped after "Incredibly blue Crater Lake."

6. Avoid clichés.

Visual clichés abound in brochures and
mailing pieces. The smiling chef appears in every
hotel brochure. The smiling girl in the bikini is a
fixture in travel literature. An intent student
peering into a microscope seems obligatory for
college catalogs.

Root out these tired illustrations. Stamp out
verbal clichés, as well.

It is much harder work to produce big *new*
ideas of your own than to borrow old ones. But
that hard work pays.

*Cooper Union's award-winning catalog
avoided visual clichés through the use of
extreme closeups. Designer Herb Lubalin
drew attention to the more than century-old
building with photographs of architectural
detail: a gargoyle, a doorknob, a stair rail.*

7. Don't be afraid of long copy.

Consumers are hungry for information, especially if they are buying a big-ticket item, such
as a vacation, or a college education. If they have
bothered to write for your brochure, or picked it

20

off a rack, they are prospects for the product or service you are selling. Tell them everything they need to know.

Bucknell University redesigned "Bucknell in Brief," its basic admissions piece, to be far less brief. The introduction alone, a thoughtful essay written by the University's philosopher-president, runs to 2,500 words. Bucknell's applications rose 10 percent after the new brochure went into use!

8. Spotlight the important facts.

Remember that one of the most frequent criticisms of brochures in general is that they "do not give enough facts." Tell consumers what is included, what are the costs, what are the hours. Graphic devices can help to spotlight important information.

Hilton Hotels' "Pleasure Chest," a guide to Caribbean package tours, uses bullets, bold type and an easy grid to list prices, This information is in the same place on every single page.

9. Use photographs instead of drawings.

Research says that photographs increase recall 26 percent over drawings. Further, photographs suggest reality and stir the reader's imagination as drawings cannot.

10. Be helpful, not clever.

Avoid gimmicky layouts and humorous copy—unless the humor contributes to the sale.

Give the consumer practical, useful information: what sort of clothing to bring on a vacation; what lodging accommodations are in your area; whether ties are required in your hotel dining room; what other attractions are available.

Above all, tell him how much money he will need to spend.

The Holland America Line discovered cruise passengers were confused about stateroom costs and locations. For its next brochure, the line prepared detailed diagrams indicating the location, size and facilities of every room on each deck. Passengers know exactly what they are buying.

11. Make your brochure worth keeping.

Give your piece longer life, and longer selling power, by encouraging the consumer to keep it handy. Travel brochures that unfold into maps are one example. Yearly calendars of events are another.

The Hudson River Museum in Yonkers, New York, made their membership mailing piece more attractive by designing it to unfold into a delightful poster, suitable for framing.

12. Give your product a first-class ticket.

Don't stint on quality. In many cases, the brochure *is* your product; the salesman who represents you in the consumer's home. The cheapest route may end up being the most costly one if it loses you a customer.

If your budget is limited, consider doing a smaller piece, one with fewer pages, or even an elegant black-and-white piece instead of four-color. Many effective brochures use color for the cover, and black and white inside. Use of two colors throughout is another alternative.

Inexpensive pieces can be just as effective as expensive ones. Charles Lamb once wrote: "The better a book is, the less it demands from binding." A statement true today.

13. Tell the truth.

This rule goes beyond purely legal requirements. Today's consumers want the truth, and the *whole* truth. They want to know your possible drawbacks, as well as your advantages.

Surprising as it sounds, disclosing your negative aspects can work in your favor.

> *American Express pioneered a brochure program that not only gave complete facts to potential travelers, but disclosed possible drawbacks. They described one tour, for example, as not suited for people unable to walk long distances. A flood of letters told them such advice made the rest of their statements extremely believable. Says Suzan Couch, who directed the program, "We started off telling the truth because we wanted to. We found that the added credibility was good for business."*

14. Use the envelope to deliver a message.

Whenever you are mailing a piece of literature, use the envelope to advantage. Tease the reader, whet his appetite, promise him a benefit for reading on.

> *The John Drew summer theater on Long Island mails brochures in May. The envelope promises: "Subscribe Now! See 4 plays for as little as $22.00." Since they started offering a benefit on the envelope, the theater has tripled subscriptions.*

15. Ask for the order.
What action do you want the reader to take? Write, telephone, see a travel agent, send a check? Every folder must contain a clear call to action. It is astonishing how many pieces fail to ask for the order.

Follow these rules—especially the first one—and you will have a more effective brochure. Finally, once you understand what usually works and what usually does not, feel free to break the rules for good reason.

Fishing
in Tennessee

Golfing
in Tennessee

We've got a lot in store for you.

We've got a lot in store for you.

Develop a "campaign look" and use it throughout your literature.

This Busch Gardens brochure shows the added drama of letting one good photo dominate the page.

CHAPTER III

The Layman's Guide to Better Layout

Milton Glaser, one of the most influential graphics designers working today, says that the key to good design is *clarity.* "You are essentially aiding in the perception of content, or amplifying content, or dramatizing content in an attempt to clarify ideas and make them more comprehensible." Good design aids communication.

The following guidelines for overall layout, typography and photography have been suggested by Glaser and other experts.

Size, Shape and Stock

Decisions on the size of your piece, the shape and number of pages and the type of paper to be used will affect every aspect of layout. These decisions must be made first.

1. Make the size appropriate to the use.

"Rack-size" brochures (such as those most used by travel agents) are usually four by nine inches. They can be mailed in a number-ten envelope. Larger brochures, eight and a half by eleven inches, for instance, can also be mailed in a standard envelope.

A brochure of unusual size will probably require special envelopes. Will your budget allow you this luxury?

2. Some shapes impose size limits.

If you can plan the type of piece that unfolds into one large page, the experts say that a total of eight panels or sixteen pages is the limit.

For a parallel-folded (or accordion-pleated) publication, don't exceed five or six folds.

3. Paper stock and paper color affect your brand image.

Glossy paper and electric colors suggest a sleek, modern image. Textured paper and a subdued palette convey richness, dignity and tradition. Choose the type of paper and the color that most enhances the image you want to communicate.

> *The Canadian province of New Brunswick wanted to convey a personality of old-fashioned serenity. They selected a coated stock, with a light-brown, lined finish that suggests a weathered clapboard.*

Overall Layout

"Develop a form that is appropriate for your use," Milton Glaser suggests. "Sometimes that means it should *not* be beautiful. A brochure about plumbing fixtures should look very different from a museum catalog."

1. Keep it simple.

A reader "enters" an attractive layout as if walking into an uncluttered room. Allow white

28

space to soothe his mind and rest his eyes. Avoid the temptation to pack every inch with pictures or with copy.

2. Surprise the reader.

Special units, such as gatefold pages which unfold into spreads, add unexpected effects. These can be useful as well as decorative, if you want to show something like the floor plan of a convention center.

3. One photograph should dominate the page.

One good photograph is worth more than several inferior ones. A dominant element on each page adds drama and helps the reader focus.

4. Be consistent.

This suggestion may seem to contradict number two above, urging you to surprise the reader. Don't overdo. If a box with rate information appears on nine pages in the lower-left corner, the reader will expect it to be there in the same place on the tenth page.

Photography

Cliché photographs are the bugbear of most brochures, even the most professional ones. Yet with care and planning given to the subjects, there is no reason why you cannot end up with dramatic, storytelling pictures.

1. Plan a "shot list."

You know your subject matter better than any photographer. Try this professional discipline: put a "shot list"—a description of all the subjects you want photographed—in writing.

A good shot list contains all the essential details. "Sun setting over the bay as one small sailboat crosses the path of light. It silhouettes the figures in the boat, a man and a woman. (Note: They are wearing bathing suits.) The boat should be small (Sunfish, for instance), not a yacht."

Do give your photographer a chance to exercise creative judgment, as well. A professional eye can have surprising insights.

2. Each photograph should make a selling point.

Ask yourself again and again: what is *unique* about my product or service? What is *important* about it? Make certain your photographs cover both areas.

3. People are interested in people.

It pays to show scenes with people in them, rather than unpopulated still lifes. Photographs of interesting faces can add a human dimension to your institution.

4. Blow up small details for added impact.

Use a part to suggest the whole. The toe of a dancer can be more dramatic than the entire figure. A bud vase on a room-service tray may make a better statement about your service than the entire tray, complete with waiter behind it.

Four Seasons Hotels feature small, elegant objects to suggest their elegant accommodations and service. Brochures show a

silver teapot, a fine crystal wine glass, or a
basket of freshly baked dinner rolls.

5. Agree on photographic fee in advance.

Photographers usually work either by the day or by a fixed fee to cover the subjects agreed upon. (Here, a "shot list" is particularly helpful.) Expenses, such as cost of film, meals on location and transportation, are almost always additional. Some photographers will ask you to pay for an assistant.

Obviously, any special photography (aerial, underwater or crane shots, for instance) will cost more. So will sessions involving small children or animals, usually because they are more time-consuming.

Get the agreement in writing. Ask for a "buyout" of the photographs, so that you will own the negatives and have unlimited use of them. Will you want the right to use these photographs for purposes other than a brochure? If so, spell out the details in advance.

6. Stock photos can save money.

When you want an unusual or specific photograph that would be exorbitant for your own photographer to cover (a picture of the North Pole), the answer is usually a stock photo. Fees vary, depending on the type and extent of use. (Warning! Most stock houses will send you transparencies for approval. Handle with care, as you are responsible for scratching or loss, and the expenses for one-of-a-kind photos can be $1500 and even more.)

7. Get releases on the spot.

The photographer, his assistant or someone you assign must be responsible for getting releases signed by any people in the photo who can be recognized. Never assume you can find these people later; get their signatures on the spot.

8. "Classic" styles date less quickly.

Clothing, hair styles and automobile models, according to photographers, date pictures faster than anything else. There is little you can do to avoid this problem completely. Here's *one* tip: classic styles in clothing and hair can add extra years of life to a photo.

Typography

Again, *appropriate* is the appropriate word. Choose the type style that will best communicate your objectives and your image to your particular audience.

Here are some very general guidelines. However, remember that typography is an art form practiced best by experts who understand it.

1. Select typefaces for readability.

A good typeface calls attention not to itself but to the message.

Avoid "clever" or unusual typefaces unless you have a good reason to use them. There are literally hundreds of typefaces to choose from. Some are serif styles, known by a little crossbar on the tops or bottoms of certain letters. (This book is set in serif typeface.) Other faces are known as sans serif.

(This sentence is set in sans serif typeface.)

Many typographers feel that a serif face is more easily readable for text. Headlines can be set either in serif or sans serif. Generally, body copy or text set in upper and lower case is easier to read than copy set in all capital letters.

2. Don't mix typefaces.

Unless you are an expert typographer, you are better off staying within the same typeface "family" for any one publication. You can use the same typeface with different weights—medium, bold, demi-bold—for different purposes within the brochure.

One elegant series of brochures designed by Milton Glaser always uses a typeface called Bookman throughout. Headlines are Bookman 48-point; body copy Bookman 10-point; subheads 6-point.

3. Avoid type smaller than 8 points.

The text of this book is set in Times Roman 11-point type. Most books for general readers are set in 10-point or larger.

(This sentence is set in 6-point type.)

You can see it is more difficult to read. Magazines tend to range from 8-point to 11-point. As a rule of thumb, if additional information or new artwork must be added to a layout, cut copy rather than reduce the size of the type.

Special readers may impose special demands. Many cruise lines, whose target audiences tend to be older, set their texts in 12-point type.

Different typefaces have different degrees of readability, regardless of size.

4. Avoid printing long copy in reverse type.

When copy is brief, reverse type (white type on a color) can produce dramatic effects. Long copy printed in this way is tedious, and reduces readership.

Printing a *headline* in reverse type, on the other hand, is now accepted practice.

To conclude with another Glaser quotation: "Graphic design is simply a method of transferring information from one point to another, but so structuring it that it produces the result you want."

SAN ANTONIO

OTTAWA

Four Seasons Plaza Nacional

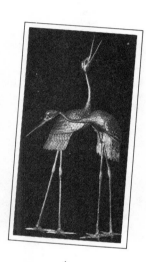

Four
Seasons
Hotel

The part can suggest the whole. Blow up small details for big impact.

Trains and
tortoises to ride.
Brahmas,
bravos and
Buggyauts.

Rollicking South Dakota.

Special effects can add impact to a layout. This one is called "silhouetting."

CHAPTER IV

How to Get Better Production

The key to better production—at lower cost—is simply *planning.* Allow 120 days from start of creative work to delivery of finished product from the printer.

The best-looking brochures are the results of care given to the layout, the copywriting, the choice of photographs. (If you want to show winter scenes in a piece that comes off the press in October, you will have to take those photographs the winter *before.*)

When production costs run over budget, *overtime* is usually the cause. Most overages can be prevented by allowing ample time for each phase: photography, retouching, typesetting, proofreading, engraving and printing.

This chapter will give you a brief guide to production. It will point out some of the errors most commonly made and suggest ways to cut production costs.

Ten Ways to Save Money on Production

1. Rely on the experts.

It pays to use professionals. A good art director can save you money and give you a better product.

A printer who understands your needs and the size of your budget is worth his weight in gold.

2. Consider asking for three print bids.

Unless you have a relative in the printing business, or a longtime working relationship, get bids from three reputable printers. (They should, of course, have comparable equipment. It would not be practical to get bids from a large web-press printer for a small job, or from a small sheet-fed printer for a large one. Be sure the printer has the right equipment for *your* job.) You are not bound to select the lowest bid, but the process assures you of paying a fair price.

> *In order to ask for bids, you must draw up specifications that will tell the printer the size of your brochure, number of pages, weight and type of paper stock, how many colors will be used and number of color photographs that will be included.*

Bidding is a discipline that makes you focus on the elements of your brochure.

3. Put a production schedule in writing.

Allow sixteen weeks from start of production to delivery. The schedule should outline each step in the process and serve to alert you when overtime threatens.

Include dates for approval of copy and layout, selection of photographs, preparation of mechanicals, delivery to printer, first proof from printer, press approvals and distribution.

Include time for correction between every

step. Copy may have to be rewritten; photographs may need retouching. *Don't* assume everything will be right the first time.

4. Order paper early.

The single biggest cost for most jobs is the printer's order of paper. Since paper costs seem to rise constantly, the earlier the printer can order, the more you save—and know you can count on the type of paper you want.

Given enough time, a printer can check several sources for the best paper buy—another economy. When ordering paper, think ahead.

If you know you will have to revise your brochure in six months (for rate and schedule changes, for example), order the paper for the second run when you make the original order.

5. Approve copy before setting type.

Resetting type because of major changes is the biggest waste of money in all brochure production. You can probably save 15 percent or more of typesetting charges by stern rules for approval!

Read copy carefully for content and spelling while it is still in manuscript. The time for change is at this stage, not after it has been set. Get legal approvals, if they are necessary, early.

> *If a number of people must read copy, ask them to sign the manuscript as an indication of approval. This little trick assures you of their attention.*

Of course, copy must be proofread *after* it has

been set, as well. Revisions, however, should be minor and due chiefly to any printer's errors—which you don't pay for—or re-editing to accommodate changes in layout.

6. Make changes on the mechanical, not the plate.

The mechanical is, quite simply, a clear indication of what the printed page will look like. The type has been set, and the type proofs are pasted down. The area for the artwork is indicated. (Sometimes a photostat the size of the actual art is pasted into position.) The original artwork to be used by the printer is attached.

> *A mechanical usually has a tissue overlay. Use the tissue to indicate any corrections; don't write on the mechanical. If you must make changes, make them now, before the material goes to the printer. Once material has been engraved, changes are extremely expensive.*

7. Transparencies give better color results than photographs.

Whenever possible, give the printer four-color transparencies (in laymen's terms, these are simply film or slides) rather than photographs. Following this rule will give you better quality; it can also minimize time-consuming—and expensive—color correction by the printer.

> *The printer or color separator will always try to match the colors in the transparency as closely as possible. If the snow in the transparency is white, you will have white*

snow in the final printed picture. Should you happen to prefer blue snow, the printer will probably charge you for color correcting. If you want colors changed, or made lighter or darker, note the request along with the transparency. Color quality is a matter of individual taste. It pays to talk things over face to face.

For a black-and-white halftone, the best material to furnish the printer is a black-and-white photograph. If color transparencies must be used, convert them to black-and-white photographs first and make sure they are acceptable before sending them to the printer.

8. Lots of small photographs mean larger production costs.

A page with one large photograph is less expensive to produce than a page with several small ones. Each color photograph must be "separated"; so the more you use, the more you pay.

To print a four-color photograph, four separate plates of the photographs are prepared, one each for yellow, red, blue and black. This "four-color process" printing reproduces the photograph.

A page with several black-and-whites will also be more costly than a page with only one.

9. Allow for "special effects" in your budget.

Special page units and unusual use of photography can add impact. They can also be expensive, so you must plan for them in your budget.

If a man is standing in front of a barn, and you want to get rid of the barn and show just the outline of the man, it is called "silhouetting." The barn is simply painted out in the original art. Many other photographic techniques are available—all at a price.

10. Think about delivery costs.

The weight of your brochure is an important consideration. Do you want to be able to afford to mail it first class? Or would you prefer to have a larger, heavier piece, even if you must settle for third-class mailing?

Will any other material be included along with the brochure? If the answer is "yes," you must allow for *that* weight, too, even if it is only a letter. Check with the post office.

The chief message of this chapter is a simple one. The more time you provide for planning, the more days you build into your schedule, the more money you will save.

Use photographs that stretch the imagination of the readers and put them in the picture.

arlington park towers
Chicago's new suburban hotel

The only hotel in the world with its own race track and golf course.

(Courtesy: Gardner, Stein & Frank, Chicago)

The most important rule of all: put your basic selling position on the cover.

CHAPTER V

More Effective Hotel Brochures

The fabled Grossinger's produces dozens of different brochures aimed at different audiences: repeat customers, honeymooners, families, singles, golf and tennis players, convention planners and more. Yet each grows out of Grossinger's positioning: *the hotel with a tradition of family hospitality.* Beneath this umbrella, various pieces can add extra emphasis to appropriate points.

Hotels and motels in the United States alone spend $30 million on brochures every year. Yet most lack a positioning, a big idea, a strong selling proposition that sets them apart from the competition. Decide on the most important benefit your hotel has to offer; then communicate it in every piece of literature you give out.

Fifteen Ways to Better Hotel Literature

1. Put your name and location on the cover.

Most travelers choose a destination first, a hotel second. Flag your customer by proclaiming your name and location boldly on the cover. Many hotels rely on their names alone; yet few are famous enough to carry this off. Some hotels settle for just a photograph on the cover. A waste of money.

2. Put your selling message on the cover.

The cover of your brochure should establish your positioning and your unique advantage.

The Whitehall Hotel in Houston sets itself apart with this positioning statement: "Welcome to the only four-star heart of Houston hotel." Since the Whitehall began using this selling message, its occupancy rate has increased 15 percent.

3. Promise the consumer a benefit on the cover.

Research says that brochures which promise the consumer something work harder than those which do not. Yet few hotel brochures bother to do this.

Consumers are selfish. Don't tell them how good you are; tell them how good the hotel will be for them.

One Omni Hotel promised: "At the Omni Hotel in Norfolk, you can sleep on the water."

Of course, the consumer benefit must be meaningful and important. The Omni Hotel knows that its waterfront location is a desirable one that gives it a march on the competition.

4. Identify your target audience on the cover.

If your brochure is talking to a particular audience, single them out on the brochure cover. Business travelers. Honeymooners. Golfers. Meeting planners.

"Six common convention complaints and

how Indies Inn cures every one." In that
cover headline, Indies Inn not only selects
its target audience, the meeting planner, but
states an important benefit.

5. The brochure must reflect your personality.

A sleek, contemporary mailing piece is just right for a sleek, modern hotel. It would be all wrong for a quiet, hundred-year-old inn which promises tradition.

Does your hotel have a personality? If so, what is it? Are you the most convenient choice for business travelers; the utmost in luxury; or the best for economical family holidays? Decide. You cannot be all of them.

6. Avoid the smiling chef and other clichés.

Open almost any hotel brochure, and you will find a photograph of a smiling chef, complete with white toque, presiding over a buffet table. Most brochures also include the grinning bellman, the happy waiter and the couple posed in the bedroom.

Eliminate these photographs, and strive for freshness.

7. Photographs can help to stretch the reader's imagination.

Allow readers to put themselves into the picture. Often, it pays to visualize what can be seen *near* your hotel, not just within it.

The brochure for Sheraton's Nile cruises
shows far more than the comfort of the
cruise ships. Photos of temples, Egyptian

wall paintings and scenes of the river
suggest what the traveler will experience.

8. Demonstrate your point of difference.

Television commercials make telling and believable points with demonstrations. This is a successful technique you can borrow.

The brochure for Del Webb's Town House Hotel does not merely describe the huge convention hall. Enormous trailer trucks were driven into it, and a photograph was taken to make the point visually. It is a powerful demonstration of the dimensions of this convention facility.

9. Show activities, not just scenery.

Don't just show your swimming pool; show people swimming in it. Don't just show your discotheque; show people dancing in it. People are interested in people.

10. Photograph food in closeup.

The exception to the rule above is food. Research says food is more appealing when shown in closeup. And always show the finished dish, not the raw ingredients.

11. Make picture captions sell your product.

You have already read that, next to the cover of the brochure, picture captions are the best-read element. Yet most hotel brochures ignore this remarkable sales aid.

Kiawah Island Hotel captions every photo with informative, competitive material.

"Historic Charleston, just 21 miles away,"
appears beneath a charming photograph of
that city. "Plan a crabbing or fishing
safari," suggests another caption, indicating
some of the activities available.

12. Maps get high readership.

Most travelers love maps. They are not only another way of giving important facts but can be used as a welcome graphic element. You might want to show exactly where your hotel is located in a city and indicate how close it is to other important sights, shopping or transportation.

The Bristol Hotel in London always includes
a map showing it is just around the corner
from Piccadilly. The Hay Adams Hotel of
Washington, D.C., never forgets to tell
consumers it has a view of the White House.

Resort hotels can give helpful information by using maps to show the layout of the resort itself.

Maps in a Ponte Vedra Club brochure depict
both the club's layout (golf course, cottages,
barber shop) and its location within the
United States.

Maps are also helpful to the many hotel visitors who arrive by car, even in big cities. Several New York City hotels include maps that show their location in relation to various bridges and tunnels into the city.

13. Give the reader helpful information.

You are asking many readers to patronize

your hotel sight unseen. The copy you include in your brochure may be the only information they have. Tell them what to bring, what to wear, what attractions are available in your area.

14. Use the brochure to be helpful to special audiences.

You do not usually have time or space in advertising to appeal to smaller "subsegments" of potential customers. Do this important job in a brochure.

Women traveling on business represent over twelve million person-nights for hotels and motels. To appeal to this growing number, consider showing a photograph of a woman checking in, with attaché case in hand. Or, to indicate that your dining room welcomes women alone, use a photograph of an unescorted woman having a pleasant dinner.

> *Western International hired a woman's travel consultant and conducted research which led them to add some simple features that appeal to women—skirt hangers, retractable clotheslines, full-length mirrors and better bathroom lighting for makeup. They advertise these features in their brochures.*

Other special segments you can address include families traveling with children. Spell out any special recreational areas or opportunities for youngsters. Potential visitors from overseas will be more likely to choose your hotel over your

50

competition if you indicate in your brochure what languages are spoken.

15. Be alert to changing life-styles.

What is happening in the world must affect every aspect of your hotel business and be reflected in your brochure.

People are eating lighter meals, vegetarian meals and health foods. If such food is available in your dining room, why not replicate a menu in your brochure?

Exercise is in. If you have an exercise room, a swimming pool or a sauna, mention it in the literature. Photograph it.

Jogging is in. If your hotel is situated in an area where jogging is possible, indicate it. (You can even include a map.)

Sixty percent of all Americans go on picnics every year. Do you pack a picnic lunch? *Do you promote that fact?*

Don't worry if a good point about your hotel (such as a nice location) is shared by your competition across the street. You still reap the benefit if your brochure talks about it, and his does not. Preempting the truth is a technique that works very well in advertising. Use it in your brochures to the same good effect.

Let us dispel the myth that positioning is only for large properties or chains. It is just as important for the small unit operator, perhaps more

51

important. *The right positioning, executed with consistency, makes every dollar work harder.*

The best positioning is a simple one, so the complexities of the hotel industry make the decision especially difficult. Promote substrategies if you must (weekday versus weekend business, for instance), but do so under one *umbrella.*

Your positioning is the motivation for a consumer to choose your property rather than another. Arriving at the right one is hard work, but it will pay off on the bottom line.

Main Photo — Big Horn Canyon in southeast Montana — one of America's most scenic recreation areas. 1. Expect to see a wide variety of uncommon wildlife, like a majestic Rocky Mountain goat. 2. Golden sunrise among the peaks of the Bitterroots start another summer day at Lake Como. 3. Wind and water have created the dramatic badlands of Makoshika State Park in eastern Montana. 4. Explore southwest Montana's Lewis and Clark Caverns — the nation's third largest.

2

3

Always use captions to identify photographs. They can be beneath the photo or keyed numerically.

Most vacationers in the United States today travel by car. Can you flag this special market?

CHAPTER VI

How to Attract More Tourists

Identify the most appealing aspect of your destination, and feature it in your literature.

Research showed that New York State's greatest appeal lay in its outdoor beauty—mountains, lakes and beaches. So the cover of the state's brochures, and most of the photographs inside, are devoted to outdoor scenes.

Too many tourism pieces attempt to list *everything* the destination offers in travelogue style. Such brochures end up looking exactly like every brochure. *Be single-minded.*

Sixteen Rules for Better Travel Brochures

1. Use the envelope to flag the reader's attention.

Travel agents throw away 34 percent of all the literature they receive without ever opening the envelope. The envelope is your first—and often last—chance to interest the prospect. Every one sent without a provocative or persuasive message is wasted.

> *Montana splashes its big mailing envelope with lavish color photographs of mountains and lakes. Expensive, but worth it in added interest.*

55

2. Use the cover to set yourself apart.

Re-read Chapter II for the basic rules for better brochures. Too many travel brochures ignore the importance of positioning the destination or giving the consumer a benefit on the cover. Never use "blind" covers that have a photograph only.

> *Grand Bahama Island positions itself on the cover with the statement, "Come play on the adult island," and the delightful illustration of a palm tree laden with dice instead of coconuts.*

3. Invite the consumer to send for more information.

Every mailing should include an invitation for the reader to send for more specifics. A prospect truly interested in your destination is your best target.

> *The State of Virginia always includes a postcard asking: "Need more Virginia travel information?" Consumers are invited to list their specific interests or destinations within the state.*

Some enlightened governmental bodies provide names of interested tourists to regional tourism groups, specific attractions and other facilities within their areas.

4. Include several pieces in a mailing.

Keep literature up-to-date without constant revision of your basic guidebook. Include separate (and less elaborate) pieces on seasonal events, available packages and rates, and basic accommodations.

> *South Carolina's "Trip Kit" includes an accommodations directory, state map, specialized brochures on camping, golf, tennis and points of interest, a calendar of events and a thank-you note.*

Don't hesitate to send inexpensive information that might produce more tourists—and tourism income.

> *Connecticut's mailing provides a simple typed list of information on shore properties for sale or rent.*

5. Include an index.

Make it easy for the consumer to use your literature. The rule of thumb is that any brochure over twenty pages must include an alphabetized index with as much detail as necessary.

6. Spotlight important information.

Remember, many consumers complain that travel brochures bury the facts. Use any graphic means—boxes, bullets, boldface type—to call attention to information the reader needs. It helps to put the same type of information, such as rates and dates, in a box that appears in the same place on every page.

7. Maps are worth their weight in gold.

Travelers love maps. Use maps to show where your destination is located, or to show tourists what to see and do within your area.

The Dominican Republic uses several maps within one brochure. Since many readers are not sure exactly where in the Caribbean the republic is located, one map shows its relationship to other, more familiar islands. Another shows major points of interest around the Dominican Republic itself.

8. "Romance maps" do triple duty.

Maps that use descriptive drawings (often humorous or romantic in nature) accomplish several objectives. They are informative, of course. They help whet the visual appetite of the traveler. And the very nature of the drawings adds a sense of personality to the destination.

Massachusetts sends a big (twenty-two-by-thirty-four-inch) colorful map studded with charming drawings that suggest the sights and activities of the state. An artist at his easel for Provincetown, the Mayflower in full sail at Plymouth Rock, covered bridges, Paul Revere, churches and statues, history and golf, entertainment and culture.

9. Show natives, not tourists.

People do not want to travel great distances to look at other people just like themselves. The United States Travel Service discovered that European visitors to the United States are not greatly interested in things they can see right at home. They want to see some purely American attractions Europe does not provide: cowboys and Indians, for instance. Or Broadway shows.

> *South Dakota's guidebook takes full advantage of its history and studs the pages with photos of ghost towns, old military posts, buffalo herds and cowboys on bucking broncos.*

Tourists want to see what they have heard about all their lives. The most effective illustration for a piece on France is still the Eiffel Tower.

10. Be helpful, not clever.

Consumers want to know what clothing to bring, what local customs dictate, what the weather will be like. Tell them where they can stay, eat, shop and sightsee.

> *The state of Alaska recognizes that a trip there is hardly an overnight impulse. Their big travel guide is packed with information that helps the traveler plan a complete vacation. It includes sections not only on all parts of the state, but on photographic safaris, river touring, sportfishing, guides and outfitters, and even instructions on how to ship your car by water.*

11. Think of new ways to give information.

All the facts need not be packed into body copy. There are refreshing ways to tell the reader what he wants to know.

> *The Canadian Government includes a two-page spread: "The twenty most commonly asked questions about Canada." It covers*

queries about subjects from liters and
celsius to Mounties.

12. Be helpful to car travelers.

The majority of vacationers in the United States still travel by car. While almost every state issues a free road map, some go further in special literature aimed at driving travelers.

New York State published a separate brochure with ten suggested vacations, each including "more to see and do than most countries," even on a single tankful of gas. Specific route instructions and maps of the itineraries were included.

13. Walking tours have new popularity.

The nineteenth-century walking tour is enjoying a new vogue, perhaps due to the increased interest in physical fitness. Be sure to include sights of interest along the route, restaurants or coffee shops, and—an essential—the mileage.

The National Tourist Office of the Netherlands has walking-tour maps for thirty historic cities and towns. They are packed with information on famous landmarks. Three tours alone include 6,000 sights!

These leisurely walks can entice tourists into staying in your area longer.

14. Appeal to children.

Typical summer vacations still include children, who can be a vocal and important factor in

60

destination choice. What can you do to appeal to them? Mention attractions and events that youngsters will enjoy.

Georgia publishes a brochure called "10 Hot Spots for Kids." It suggests, among other things, the Atlanta Zoo, the alligators in Okefenokee Swamp and a visit to a Creek Indian Village.

15. Stress value.

People will not deprive themselves of a vacation because of rising prices. They will, however, demand value for the money. *Tell them what they can get free, or for very little money, or for less than they can buy it elsewhere.*

The British Travel Association presents the joys of inexpensive holidays in Britain, from free sights such as the Changing of the Guard, inexpensive pub lunches and bed-and-breakfast accommodations to the fact that Georgian silver and cashmere sweaters are a bargain.

16. Cultivate a brochure style.

A "campaign look" is just as important in travel literature as it is in travel advertising. A family resemblance reminds consumers of your other literature and makes every dollar you spend work harder. You can vary photographs on brochure covers, but use the same basic layout, type style and a consistent logo.

Tennessee uses a homely, wide-mouthed jar

as its visual umbrella, with the line: "We've got a lot in store for you." The jar with fish swimming in it is the cover for a brochure on fishing; the golfing brochure shows it filled with grass, a golf ball and tee; the brochure on accommodations uses room keys and a wine glass.

Be consistent in the messages you deliver to potential visitors. Give them all the information they need, make that information easy to absorb and you will have a better tourism brochure. Finally, tell the truth, and you will have a more satisfied tourist. And one more likely to return.

Frederic Remington Museum
303 Washington Street   Ogdensburg, New York 13669
Phone: 315-393-2425

Monday through Saturday (open all year)
10:00 a.m.-5:00 p.m.
Sunday (June through September only)
1:00 p.m.-5:00 p.m.
Closed Holidays

*Art prints, books, cards, and colored slides of Reming-
ton Masterpieces are on sale at the Museum or by mail.*

Frederic
Remington
MUSEUM

*This brochure for the Frederic Remington Museum illustrates two
important rules: use one illustration on the cover and tell the
consumer exactly where you are located.*

Every element of the brochure must communicate your "brand image" or personality.

CHAPTER VII

Promoting Theme Parks and Attractions

Knott's Berry Farm believes that, for attractions, tourism is an *area* goal. Since visitors will probably not spend more than a few hours at your particular amusement center, it is essential to tell them what else they can see and do nearby. The brochure Knott's distributes gives not only details of the Berry Farm attractions but the location of dozens of competitive attractions nearby. Knott's has increased its attendance 42 percent within two years.

Another way to take advantage of nearby competition is simply to suggest how close you are to them. Orlando's Sea World states on its brochure cover that it is just "Ten minutes from Walt Disney World."

More attractions could learn from these examples, an old story of doing well by doing good. Several guidelines are peculiar to the literature of theme parks and amusement centers; others are true for brochures in general.

Fourteen Rules for Brochures That Attract Visitors

1. Highlight new features.

Attractions thrive on *news:* rides, exhibits,

entertainment that was not there the year before and helps lure return visitors. Newsiness also gives you a competitive edge and a sense of urgency. In planning brochures, allow for annual changes that announce new features. The best place to do this is on the cover.

The Movieland Wax Museum in Buena Park, California, shows Burt Reynolds and Barbra Streisand on its brochure cover with the announcement: "New! New!" The museum changes its cover annually, featuring new figures.

2. Put your positioning on the cover.

Use the cover to tell the reader who you are, what you are and what benefit you are offering him. What makes your attraction different from any other? Tell the reader up front.

"The only musical showpark in the whole USA," says the cover of Opryland's brochure. It also carries the location of the park: Nashville, Tennessee.

Another example of positioning is seen on the cover of Great Adventure: "Drive-thru Safari. The World's Largest Outside of Africa Itself."

3. Use one photo on the cover.

One splashy picture on the cover will make your brochure leap out of the rack and invite the reader to open it.

Sea World's killer whale leaps out of the water and right at the reader. It dominates

66

the cover and suggests the excitement
waiting for visitors.

With so many features to sell, attractions are tempted to put multiple illustrations on a cover. Discipline yourself. One photo works better than many photos.

4. Involve the reader in your copy.

Copy that makes the reader feel part of the action helps motivate a visit. Be specific, not general.

> *"Encounter the Force!" begins the copy for*
> *Astro World's Greezed Lightning.*
> *"Imagine being launched, quick as*
> *lightning, to speeds of sixty miles per hour*
> *in less than four seconds. With a mind-*
> *boggling force of six G's, you orbit upside*
> *down around an enormous Texas-sized*
> *loop, circling over eighty feet into the*
> *Houston sky."*

5. Tell the reader who your visitors are.

Some theme parks are thought of as places only for teenagers seeking thrill rides. Others are considered for very young children. Tell the prospect who your usual visitors are. Portray them in the brochure, if you can.

> *Six Flags Over Texas demonstrates that the*
> *park has all-family appeal. They show a*
> *variety of tourists enjoying themselves—*
> *toddlers, teenagers, grandparents.*

6. One photograph should dominate a page.

67

You know that one photo works better than many on the cover. The same rule holds true for inside pages. A good layout gives the reader *one* important element on which to focus.

> *Busch Gardens Dark Continent brochure unfolds into a page fifteen and a half by sixteen and a half inches, which contains forty-seven different photographs. Yet one picture dominates the page: the head and neck of a giraffe, fifteen inches high.*

7. Sell romance and excitement.

Most attractions take the visitor into another world, whether it is one of fantasy, space or our own country's past. Research indicates that Americans are increasingly turning to forms of escapism. Take advantage of this trend by selling your special escape in pictures and copy. Don't be afraid of old-fashioned romance.

> *Old Tucson offers visitors a chance to ride a stagecoach, see a gunfight, have a drink at the Golden Nugget saloon. This forty-year-old attraction is, next to the Grand Canyon, the most popular tourist destination in the entire state of Arizona.*

8. Your brochure should reflect your image.

Does your theme park stand for death-defying thrill rides or wholesome family fun? The *look* and *feel* of the brochure helps communicate your personality.

> *The Publick House Restaurant in Old*

Sturbridge Village, Massachusetts,
reproduces its 1771 signpost on the cover,
makes effective use of eighteenth-century
typeface and uses down-to-earth Yankee
writing. "Come for a weekend," the copy
invites, and "we'll make hot buttered rum,
toast chestnuts, take a sleigh ride through
Old Sturbridge Village and leave the
twentieth century behind."

9. Tell people what you offer free.

Today's visitors are wary about hidden costs. Spell out exactly what guests should expect to pay. If there are special rates for children under a certain age, say so.

Walt Disney World, past master at
brochures that produce tourists, says in
bold type: "The following are
complimentary attractions."

10. Urge the reader to take action.

Use imperative verbs like "come," "enjoy," and "relax in." Invitations to act are especially effective on the cover.

"Have a Great Day at the Great Western
Winery," is more persuasive than saying
simply: "Great Western Winery." Similarly,
the literature for one of New York City's
most popular attractions urges: "See
Lincoln Center." This brochure continues
to exhort the reader to "Reserve a
Rehearsal," a special event included in the
guided tour.

11. Three attractions are better than one.

Pool your resources with other attractions in your area for a joint brochure. (Consider special joint-ticket admissions, as well.)

> *Three historical mansions in New York State banded together in one brochure called "Sleepy Hollow Country," after famous local author Washington Irving. The brochure describes all three, with a map showing how easy it is to include them all in one tour—and at one price.*

Joining forces may make it possible for you to do a more colorful, larger brochure than you could produce on your own.

12. Highlight your most popular feature.

This rule relates—again—to the major problem found in brochures for attractions. Everything is given equal emphasis; therefore nothing stands out. Put the spotlight on the feature that interests most visitors.

> *The Frederic Remington Museum houses a great collection of paintings by the well-known artist of the American West. Yet the brochure wisely shows on the cover only his most popular canvas: that of an Indian on horseback.*

13. Don't overlook the power of testimonials.

Endorsements from real people—a tried-and-true advertising technique—help to make your claims believable. Yet they are generally overlooked by attractions.

> *"Perhaps unequaled by any botanic garden in the world," declares the brochure of the Brooklyn Botanic Garden. This statement is a testimonial from the book,* Great Botanical Gardens of the World.

14. It doesn't have to be expensive to be good.
Simple black-and-white or two-color literature can stand out on a rack. Rely on ample white space and tasteful graphics.

> *The Shaker Museum in Old Chatham, N.Y. reflects the austere beliefs of the order with a brochure that is eye-catching in its simplicity. It uses blue as a second color for headlines and subheads, with simple illustrations and lots of white space.*

As many brochures today tend to grow more ornate, a simple piece can attract the reader's attention by its sheer contrast.

Take away only two *ideas from this chapter, and you will have more successful brochures. Remember that attractions, in almost every case, must help persuade tourists to visit the region, not the attraction itself. Second, decide on your most popular feature, and highlight it.*

Alan Alda
Alumnus, Fordham College

"Someday, at some point in your lives, maybe years from now, a lot of you are going to look up from your work and wonder what's the point of it all. You'll wonder how much you're really getting accomplished and how much it all means."

The statement could be that of a philosophy professor, lecturing to a group of freshmen in Keating Hall, perhaps. But our headline says Alan Alda—the actor known for his role as the rather offbeat Hawkeye Pierce on television's long-running *M.A.S.H.* series.

A graduate of Fordham College, Class of 1956, Alan Alda has become rich and famous through his portrayal of Hawkeye, but in the process he has nurtured other talents and kept his sense of what's important, what life is really all about.

He has turned his back on parts he did not believe in when he needed a job, and shunned the glitter of Hollywood for the small town of Leonia, New Jersey, where he lives with his wife and children. He is outspoken in behalf of women's rights.

The above quotation, as well as what follows, was taken from his address to Fordham students at the 1978 graduation ceremony:

"It seems to me that your life will have meaning when you can *give* meaning to it. Because no one else will give meaning to your life. There isn't a job or a title or a degree that has meaning in itself. And there isn't a liquor that will give meaning to your life—or a drug—or any type of sexual congress either.

"I'd like to suggest to you, just in case you haven't done it yet, that this would be a good time to find out what your values are—and then figure out how you're going to be able to live by them. Knowing what you care about and then devoting yourself to it is just about the only way you're going to be able to have

a sense of purpose in your life.

"Times seem to have changed quite a bit since the sixties. In those days everyone was out on the streets. But you've come in out of the street. They say you're thinking more about your own careers now than about marching.

"Well, if that's true, the funny thing is that it's possible that you can do more to change things than anyone could in the sixties.

"If you can put a high value on decency...

"If you can put a high value on excellence...

"—And on family...if you can love the people you share your lives with—your wives and your husbands and your children—and if you don't shortchange them for a few bucks...if you can love the work you do—and learn the skill of it, the art of it—and 'love your art, as poor as it may be...'

"If you can give full measure to the people who pay you for your work...

"If you can try not to lie, try not to cheat, try to do good just by doing well whatever you do...

"*Then* you will have made a revolution."

13

Make the most of your successful alumni. Fordham features its famous graduate, actor Alan Alda.

CHAPTER VIII

What Works Best in College Literature?

"College *is* a place of dreams and ideals; write up to the aspirations," suggests Dennis O'Brien, President of Bucknell University. "Writing down will not only leave the student 'where he's at'— but it is unlikely to impress father and mother. In our democratic families, students pick their college—from a list approved by their parents. A really effective admissions publication will get you on the parents' list."

The most important type of college literature is certainly that for student recruitment, followed closely by fund-raising pieces. This chapter will suggest more effective techniques for both. In addition, it will point out some guidelines that are guaranteed to cut costs.

Perhaps nowhere is competition more intense in such a short period of time as it is in the college recruitment race. Some students receive several dozen to more than one hundred pieces of literature, most of them unsolicited. Unless you stand out from the pack, your brochure will be ignored.

A study by the Barton-Gillet Company of Baltimore indicated that students look to publications for help in selecting a college, but feel they are not getting the information they need. Too many institutions are presenting themselves as all things to all people.

Here are ten rules followed by the most successful colleges, where enrollment is going *up*, not down.

Recruitment Literature

1. It pays to be candid.

A national task force revealed that widespread misperceptions about costs and courses of study were causing many students to attend the wrong schools for their needs. The results included large proportions of second-year dropouts and inevitable hard feelings.

Many institutions are now painting unusually honest pictures of their weaknesses as well as their strengths.

> *Barat College in Lake Forest, Illinois, acknowledges in its prospectus that "some students feel they don't get out, meet men and date enough." At the same time, others were quoted as praising "the friendliness of almost everyone."*

Just like truth-in-packaging, truth-in-prospectusing seems to be working. One college, reporting that the number of freshmen students transferring out had decreased by half, identified the cause. "Our admission publications are simply communicating better what we are all about."

2. Include a personalized letter in all search mail-

74

ings if you can.

Research tells us a mailing that includes a personal (or personal-appearing) cover letter explaining why the student is being solicited is far more likely to be taken seriously.

3. Get your material out early.

It is a fact that students begin to lose interest after they receive more than one dozen search mailings. Search mailings to juniors should be ready for mailing immediately after PSAT scores are received in mid-April.

4. Tout outstanding faculty and alumni.

Your impressive faculty members are a drawing card. Don't be afraid to brag about them and their achievements. Picture them. Describe their awards, books, special projects.

Warning: don't promise courses taught by distinguished professors engaged in research, not teaching.

Make much of your successful alumni. Potential students want to know that people who have made their mark in various fields are graduates of your institution. The facts are more than impressive; they suggest graduating students may be able to get some help in entering that field.

> *The Fordham University prospectus features its famous alumnus, actor Alan Alda, best known for his long-running M.A.S.H. television series. In addition, it spotlights key faculty members in many different departments.*

5. Testimonials add believability.

Use of current students, who have widely different backgrounds, interests and career ambitions, can contribute authenticity to any recruitment message.

Michigan's Delta College segmented its appeal to specific target audiences with eight different fliers. Each one focused on a representative student explaining: "Why I chose Delta." The one-color pieces cost about six cents each!

6. Use storytelling photographs.

Perhaps the worst criticism that can be aimed at recruitment publications is the use of photographic clichés: happy student under oak tree; happy professor leaning over happy student at microscope; happy participants in some form of athletics. Almost any photograph could be exchanged for one in a different college brochure without misrepresentation.

No area is worth more time and effort from the publications staff than development of an exciting and unique photo library. Here again, consider hiring a professional for a specific series. Outline for the photographer, *in writing,* exactly what pictures you want. This exercise places the burden where it belongs: on the people who best know the university.

Stroll through the campus and the buildings. Make notes for "photo opportunities." How do you want the head of the zoology department to appear: in a business suit at his desk, or working with a chimpanzee?

A famous professional photographer, asked for his advice on college brochures, said simply, "Think small, print large." Details, such as an ancient date on the cornerstone of a building, framed by ivy tendrils, can say more than a photo of the entire building.

When in doubt, use large photographs instead of small ones.

7. Make every caption set you apart.

When you fail to caption a photo, you are losing a valuable chance to communicate to your reader. Don't say: "Student using electron scanner." Say: "Student using the only electron scanner in the southeastern United States."

A study of hundreds of university pieces revealed almost no use of captions, or, at best, few that gave worthwhile information.

8. Maps are powerful tools.

Prospective students are eager to know what your campus looks like, as well as exactly where your college is located within its state. All manner of graphic devices are open to you, from realistic bird's-eye views with keys to various buildings to "romance maps," into which an illustrator can add charm or humor.

Agnes Scott College in Georgia used two different maps in its recruitment literature to solve two problems. Many potential students thought the college was extremely isolated. The solution: a simple map that indicated the school is only six miles from Atlanta. The second problem was that few students knew the college was beautiful, rural and, above all, equipped with facilities including science, fine arts and complete gymnasium. A pictorial map proved to be the simple—and successful—solution.

9. Spotlight important facts.

Make your brochure easy for the student to use. If it is a large publication, include a table of contents. Be specific and factual in your headlines. Resist cuteness.

Rutgers University, which includes more than twenty different colleges, produces a brochure with the details of each one in a separate box. "Rutgers College at a Glance" gives the reader the size, housing, faculty and type of classes.

10. Ask for the order.

A return card should always accompany original search mailings, allowing the student to ask for an interview, request more information and indicate his particular area of interest.

Fund-Raising Pieces

Academia depends for its life on fund-raising: annual giving, campaigns, grants, matching funds, bequests and the like. Every potential donor is being bombarded by similar institutions, many of

78

them with an equally good cause to claim his attention and his dollars. (Note: Although Chapter X is specifically devoted to fund-raising brochures, the special nature of college literature demands separate treatment.)

Two tried-and-true advertising methods are at work here: first, get the prospect's *attention;* then, *persuade* him to give, and to give as much as he possibly can.

1. Make your effort a series of requests.

Most professional fund raisers know they must continually press for donations. You can add impact and continuity by sending a series of mailings linked by one campaign theme.

> *Earlham College in Indiana sent out three consecutive pieces, featuring professors selected for their popularity and varied fields of study. The theme was: "Why do I teach at Earlham?" The brochures look modest; the professors' own handwriting is reproduced on notebook paper, illustrated with simple, candid snapshots. The brochures cost less than two cents each. The fund-raising drive broke all previous records.*

2. Keep it personal.

In fund raising, nothing works better than a personal solicitation. When designing brochures, consider whether hand tailoring is worth the extra expense and effort. It pays to test and find out.

> *The University of Pennsylvania has an "in-*

*house" agency which is responsible for all
publications of the many subschools. An
analysis of the fund-raising needs of Arts
and Sciences and of Medical Research led
to two distinctive and very different
brochures.*

3. Be specific about costs.

Evangelist Aimee Semple McPherson is said
to have built a church by telling members of her
congregation exactly the cost of each brick, each
pew, each hymnal. Universities could profit from
her lesson.

*The University of Maryland spells out the
cost of a permanently endowed chair, or a
distinguished professorship, while
suggesting that positions can also be created
for shorter terms at a lower cost.*

Other colleges have found it helpful to break
down a suggested gift to *daily* equivalents.
Guilford College invited its alumni to give up one
prune Danish every morning.

4. Thank your benefactor publicly.

Good manners dictate a personalized note
of thanks to each donor immediately on receipt of
his money or pledge. Good sense dictates a *public*
acknowledgment, annually, of all benefactors.

Indicate the area of giving ($1,000–$2,500,
for instance), but not the specific amount. Ac-
knowledge special funds: Association for the
Arts; Friends of the Library; Engineering Fund.

5. Zero in on matching funds potential.

The alumnus who works at a Matching Funds company is worth more to you than a classmate who contributes equally. Comb your lists for these high-yield individuals, and go after them with zeal.

> *Lafayette College sent out brochures with a provocative message on the envelope: "When was the last time an investment you made doubled, tripled or even quadrupled?"*

6. Use challenge grants in new ways.

Most institutions make use of challenge grants to stimulate broader, deeper giving. What else can you do? Give your next challenge some creative thought.

> *Haverford College challenged the challenge. They not only asked each alumnus to help them qualify by increasing his giving, they asked that each write the foundation promising an additional gift if the grant were approved. Haverford received its grant.*

Seven Guidelines for Cutting Costs

Colleges tend to proliferate printed matter aimed at both external and internal audiences: campus bulletins, alumni newsletters, events calendars, special school or departmental brochures, posters, annual reports.

Firm central supervision and financial control are keys to holding costs down. Some general rules are in order.

Seven Rules for Better (and Less Costly) College Publications

1. Weed out annually—and ruthlessly.

Avoid duplication and overlap of publications. Check to make sure that a "one-shot" flier has not turned into an annual piece, simply through oversight. Put *all* publications under the control of one office—no matter how difficult the politics—and set an annual date for spring weeding. Get the decision makers involved and ask, for every scrap of literature you print: is this piece necessary?

2. Agree on your target audience.

Once you agree the brochure is necessary, you must also know who you are talking to. The tone of voice appropriate for a fund-raising letter to alumni doctors will not work for high-school recruitment.

3. Recycle copy and photographs.

Get more for your money by making every piece of copy and every visual do at least double duty. The same photograph that you send to the wire services can serve for the campus newspaper, the alumni bulletin and the annual report.

> *Lehigh reuses the same color separations for its viewbook (which goes to prospective students) and its annual report (sent to alumni and parents). There is virtually no*

overlap of audience, and a great saving in costs.

4. Seek professional help.

Bob Beyers of Stanford, acknowledged dean of university public-relations staffs, once said: "In conflict between professional and institutional loyalties, the institution usually will be served in the long run by those whose primary loyalty is to journalistic standards."

The same rule holds for photography. Most schools interviewed for this chapter agreed that it paid to hire a professional photographer. Most had learned the lesson from bitter experience.

The Cooper Union recently turned out an award-winning magazine-style guide. The art director was famed graphic designer Herb Lubalin, an alumnus. Not all colleges are so fortunate.

Consider employing an outside designer for consultation on your overall graphic look.

5. Conduct readership studies.

How well is your material read? Send comment cards annually with your major publications. (This method also checks the accuracy of your mailing list.)

Ohio State University's Office of Public Affairs conducted a readership study among 700 readers of its new alumni newspaper, OSU Quest. *Responses helped the editor identify what readers wanted most: more articles on scientific and scholarly research.*

6. Project a unified image.

Each publication should build the image of your university. And each should bear a family resemblance to other pieces. Some helpful suggestions include: use of same typeface; logo; consistent choice of colors and similar layout of all publication covers.

This rule not only makes sense, it is a wily way to get more brand recognition for your money.

Tiny Hollins, a women's college in Virginia, was cited for the best total publications program of any U.S. college. Continuity in design is one of their top priorities. "And," notes their Director of Publications, "developing a format for specific series of publications also helps us save money, because we bid and award each series as a package."

Too many colleges waste money because their brochures do not have a consistent personality.

7. Control your costs.

First, re-read Chapter IV on how to get better production for less money. All suggestions apply to some phase of college publications.

Further, some of the following suggestions gleaned from dozens of institutions may help solve *your* particular problem.

• Set a budget for publications. And stick to it!
• Save money on internal publications. Quan-

tities are often small. Consider using an IBM executive machine to prepare the type.

• Print some color work so that a two-year or three-year supply is available. The color area remains the same; the "black plate" (or non-color area) can be changed to revise the text at little cost. This technique can work not only for brochures but for pieces such as commencement programs or annual reports.

• Consider "self-covers" for brochures so an additional press run is not required for a cover.

• When listing names, always set them from existing computer magnetic tape, if available.

• Investigate the cost saving of your own "in-house" type-setting facility. Might it pay off by work you could do for private sector jobs in your community?

Few booklets bear the enormous burden of college recruitment literature. Perhaps no environment is more competitive. Further, the consumer shops for a relatively brief period, makes only one *purchase and then goes out of the marketplace. And what other brochures have to sell a $30,000 item that will shape the entire future of the purchaser?*

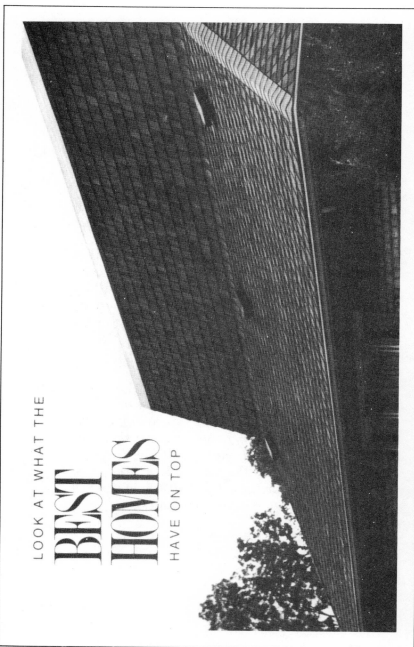

LOOK AT WHAT THE

BEST HOMES

HAVE ON TOP

Give your product or service "star quality" so consumers will see it in a first-class light.

CHAPTER IX

More Brochures— to Gain Members, to Advocate, to Persuade, to Sell

No matter what the purpose of your booklet, use the cover to advantage. Tell your story. Establish your personality. Let the reader know exactly who you are.

These seem easy suggestions to follow. Yet a study of recent brochures reveals that the more prestigious the institution, the more obscure the cover. Some covers are even left *blank!* Since four out of five readers never get beyond the cover, that wastes 80 percent of the money.

Whether you use literature to attract members, create interest in a cause or sell a product, ask yourself if it is doing the most effective job possible.

The following guidelines serve as a helpful checklist.

Twelve More Tips for Better Brochures

1. Decide on your target audience.

If you think your audience is everybody, think again. Any communication aimed at so broad a target is doomed to fail. Talk to everyone, and you reach no one.

Merrill Lynch recognized working women as an important market but realized many women were not sophisticated about finances and investments. As part of a long-term program, the company published "You and Your Money. A Financial Handbook for Women." It is packed with information on how to read stock quotations, how to reorganize finances, how to invest. Over 200,000 copies were distributed the first year.

2. Use the cover to make the reader take action.

Tell the audience what you expect them to do. Say: "Join the Jones Museum," rather than "The Jones Museum."

"Discover the Cleveland Museum of Natural History," one brochure invites on its cover. Inside, the theme is continued with "Discover History," "Discover the Exhibits" and "Discover Research."

3. Involve the reader.

Use devices that lure prospects into reading your message. Quizzes are one good example. "Ten Questions You Should Ask Before Going into the Hospital" proved an effective piece for the Hospital Council of Southern California.

The better the device fits the interests of your target audience, the harder it will work.

As part of a fire safety program, Burger King distributed brochures which contained a board game for children. The spaces

*carried instructions such as: "You
organized a fire drill at home. Go ahead
two spaces" and "Danger. Candle too near
curtain, lose one turn." It proved a
memorable way for Burger King's young
audience to learn about fire safety.*

4. Don't be afraid to be human.

Use this trick when you are writing copy (or
reviewing it). Remember you are talking to *one*
particular reader, not a faceless crowd. Visualize
that one person and talk to him. Be warm and
personal.

*"What Is Green, a Joy Forever, and Named
After You?" asks a brochure for the
Houston Parks Board. Inside, the reader
finds: "Answer. A Park in the City of
Houston." This piece was designed to
generate awareness of the need for more
park land, especially among bank trust
officers and lawyers specializing in wills and
trusts. The campaign increased the city's
parkland by over 22 percent.*

Another example of adding human interest to
otherwise dry statistics was done by the Cleveland
Museum of Natural History. It asked potential
members to "Adopt a Wet-Pet," and explained
that the reader could support anything from a
living sponge for fifty cents a week to the entire
seal exhibit for $10,000 per year.

5. Give your product "Star Quality."

Nobody likes to support a second-rate institution or invest time or money in a shabby cause. Give your product first-class treatment, and chances are consumers will perceive it in a first-class light.

> *The Asphalt Roofing Industry launched a program to increase its share of the new-home construction market. "Look At What the Best Homes Have on Top," the brochure proclaimed and illustrated the latest trends in asphalt shingles by showing homes in the $70,000-and-up range.*

6. Testimonials add believability.

Like demonstrations, testimonials have proved themselves as an effective advertising technique, yet are virtually ignored in collateral material. They can add great credibility to your claim.

Consider testimonials by experts. A professional photographer who uses your camera, for instance. Or a fashion designer who praises your fabric.

Another type of endorsement comes from "the man on the street"—a satisfied user. (Tip: use the person's own words, and avoid cosmetic surgery. Reality has powers the best copywriter cannot capture.)

A third kind is a testimonial by individuals who are recognized and respected by your audience.

> *The Nature Conservancy, a non-profit conservation organization, was established*

to encourage corporate gifts of critical natural lands. The brochure used persuasive quotations from well-known corporate executives. The program helped increase the number of corporate associates from five to over two hundred.

7. Keep your finger on the consumer's pulse.

"Junk mail" has been defined, simply, as any mail that particular customer isn't interested in. Know what interests your target audience, and address it in your literature. You reduce the chances of having your brochure thrown away by at least 50 percent!

The architectural firm of Haines Lundberg Waehler knew its client companies were vitally concerned with the issue of energy-efficient buildings. In a piece entitled "Energy Opportunities," the firm gave specific case histories showing how energy was saved for both new buildings and renovated structures.

8. Monitor the effectiveness of your material.

Is your brochure really working? Always include some way for the consumer to respond, whether through an address, a telephone number or a reply card. It pays, now and then, to use a bounce-back device or premium to find out if the consumer is responding to your message.

9. It doesn't have to be expensive to be good.

A simple black-and-white or two-color leaflet, if well done, can work as hard as a glossy four-color piece. What you say is more important than how you say it.

For years, International Ballet competitions were dominated by Eastern European countries. The first United States International Ballet Competition, hosted by Jackson, Mississippi, attracted sixty-four dancers from fourteen countries. The brochure was only a two-color piece, with effective use of a red logo and red headlines to attract the reader's attention.

10. Pool your efforts.

Earlier, you read that theme parks and other attractions are learning it is profitable to join forces. Working with other products or institutions can stretch your dollars and make your literature available to a larger audience.

The Smithsonian "takes its show on the road" every year. It brings programs to host museums in selected cities. Brochures are sent directly from Washington to Smithsonian Associates in these cities and are bulk-mailed to the local organizations. Both parent and host organizations gain from the program. One co-sponsoring museum signed up over 500 new members within two months of the series. And the Smithsonian, which receives from 3 percent to 10 percent response to its brochure mailing, keeps in touch with its own membership.

11. Announce news.

Don't bury news about yourself. Always think, when you are preparing a brochure, about the possibility of touting a new feature or a new accomplishment.

You can do this inexpensively, by making changes on the black plate only. Or simply add an announcement (Now in four new colors!) to the existing cover.

The Children's Museum in Indianapolis produced a simple two-color leaflet to announce the news of a planned gallery of Physical Science and to solicit contributions. The Museum raised more than its goal of $200,000.

12. Use the envelope to advantage.

When mailing brochures, always put a message on the envelope. Remember, you have only seconds to get the reader's attention, or have your mailing thrown away. If you are offering something of value inside, say so on the outside.

"A select number of men and women are being invited this year to become members," states the envelope for a mailing by the American Museum of Natural History. "You are one of the chosen. Exceptional benefits include a subscription to Natural History Magazine." Using the envelope to good advantage helped this membership mailing beat the previous one by a whopping 35 percent.

A word about testing. If your brochure is a one-time-only effort, you must rely on your own judgment and the guidelines in this book for what usually works and what usually does not. For on-going programs (membership drives, for example) it pays to test. Set up different cells and test premium offers, test brochure covers, test varied messages outside. Try to beat your own record with each mailing.

Both your language and your graphics should appeal to your target audience. In this case, children.

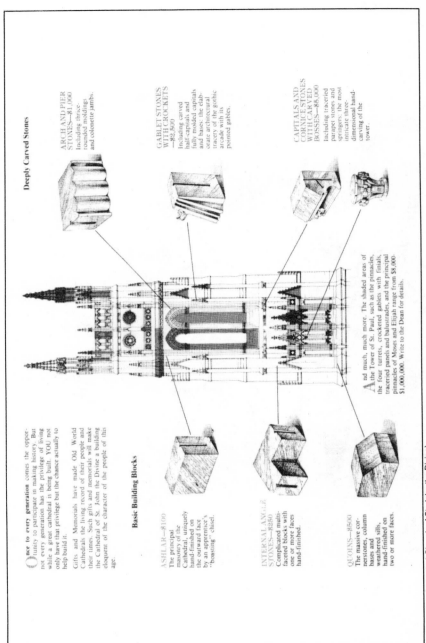

(Courtesy: The Cathedral Church of St. John the Divine)

Tell prospects exactly what their dollar will buy, whether a meal for a child or a building stone.

CHAPTER X

How to Do More Effective Fund-Raising Literature

The great professional fund-raiser Harold J. Seymour once said that every cause needs people more than money. No letter, no brochure can replace personal attention and solicitation.

This chapter, however, will not attempt to discuss in detail the intricacies of fund raising, such as planning, goals, recruitment, quotas and so on. Entire books have been devoted to the subject. These pages will simply list some guidelines that help fund-raising letters and brochures perform better.

Before You Start the Campaign

A good fund-raising campaign, like a good advertising campaign, needs a strategy. Decide on your objective, target audience, consumer benefit and support for that benefit. The "personality" of your appeal must fit the image of the cause.

The Girl Scout Council of Greater New York decided to expand its summer camp facilities. The fund-raising staff was aware that many donors wish to help underprivileged girls get away from the city in the summer. The Council adopted the following strategy:

97

1. Objective—to raise $20,000 for construction of facilities to house forty more Girl Scouts at summer camp.

2. Target audience—small givers who might make contributions of $250 or more for two reasons: the personal appeal of the cause, and the year-end timing of the request which made a tax deduction possible in either year.

3. Consumer benefit—the satisfactions of helping to send an underprivileged city girl to summer camp.

4. Support—acknowledgement of donor's name in a book of specially drawn Girl Scout cartoons, widely distributed.

5. Tone and manner—warm and persuasive, in keeping with the image of Girl Scouting.

This "Gold Book" of cartoons was the idea of a well-known New Yorker, Mrs. John A. Morris, who solicited donations by letters and in person. The appeal—and the book—were so successful they have become a fixture of Council fund raising.

Guidelines for Fund-Raising Letters and Brochures

1. Gear the message to the target audience.

A letter that motivates the small giver is probably not the right one for a major giver. Large donors tend to need information; small donors will heed an emotional appeal.

A New York Hospital mailing spoke of

four patients who owe their lives to the hospital: a baby, a young girl, a businessman and an elderly woman. The letter concluded: "Our foremost concern for the past 200 years has been people, their lives and health. I believe you share that concern." This emotional appeal evoked greater response than those which dealt in statistics.

2. Premiums can help.

Many fund-raising campaigns rely on the offer of useful or desirable premiums. The American Red Cross constantly tests appeal letters. The letter offering the free Standard First Aid Manual consistently receives the best response.

Often these premiums can be unique: items made available only to donors.

Public Television's Channel Thirteen offered former members a folding umbrella with the station logo for rejoining with a twenty-five-dollar membership. The umbrella, which cannot be purchased commercially, tells the world that its owner supports Thirteen. So this premium generates awareness as well as funds.

3. The premium should fit your image.

The best premiums reflect the personality of the cause. The Metropolitan Museum of Art rewards membership contributions with handsome books illustrating special exhibitions.

4. "Obligation Devices" increase response.

When a respondent gets something for nothing, he may feel obligated enough to make a contribution. The Christmas Seals of the National Tuberculosis and Respiratory Diseases Association are the classic obligation device of all time. Mailings with the seals raise approximately $45 million annually.

The Republican National Party sends registered party members a plastic membership card. The message states: "We know you are going to be a dues-paying member." This assumptive device helped build a membership of one-half million Republicans who pay annual dues.

5. It pays to personalize.

A personal salutation is more effective than "Dear friend." Specific references make the contributor feel you recognize him as a *person*. A hospital appeal that recognizes a woman's interest in the pediatric clinic, a university mailing that acknowledges an alumnus is an engineer—both will fare better than impersonal requests. How far you carry this depends on your budget and the sophistication of your equipment.

Another effective technique is personalizing an obligation device.

The Disabled American Veterans for many years sent out miniature replicas of respondents' license plates for use as identification tags. It proved extremely successful. Now this organization sends one hundred name-and-address stickers with each appeal letter. This device achieves the same level of response as the license plates—at a lower cost!

6. Ask for a specific amount of money.

Never leave the contribution amount up to the individual. Specify how much you hope he will give, or what others of his standing have already given. Professionals suggest you begin by suggesting *larger amounts first,* then moving to smaller sums.

The United Way has long used an effective means of guiding contributions. They have a "Fair Share" brochure which lists what other people in a similar salary range have given. United Way also suggests payroll deductions spread throughout the year, which tend to result in higher contributions.

When dealing with past donors, tell them what they gave the last time and ask them to increase the gift. Chances are they will do so.

7. Avoid "Two-Step" appeals.

These appeals begin by asking for a *small* amount of money, in return for which more information is sent. A follow-up letter then solicits the prospect for a larger gift. Many fund raisers have tried "two-step" approaches in hopes that a knowledgable contributor will be a generous contributor. Unfortunately, the technique seldom works.

8. Keep your contributors involved in your cause.

This rule is a fairly easy one to follow if an annual contribution includes active membership, as in the case of a museum. Direct contact with the cause raises contribution levels. Bucknell University discovered there is a direct correlation between level of giving and return visits to campus. If you must, *invent* ways to keep in touch with contributors.

> *The research libraries of the New York Public Library recognized the necessity of keeping member-contributors involved. The staff created a quarterly newsletter, "Library Lines," which costs only a few cents per member annually. The membership has risen in five years from 5,000 to 40,000.*

9. Tell donors exactly what their dollar is buying.
People think in specifics, rather than generalities. Save the Children for many years successfully asked for *specific* amounts of money. Fifty dollars can provide meals for an entire school class.

> *The Cathedral of St. John the Divine tested two approaches with a split-run magazine advertisement. One headline was a general appeal. The winning advertisement promised: "Give us an ashlar, internal angle stone, quoin, arch, pier, gablet, capital or cornice stone . . . and we'll give you a Cathedral." The various stones were pictured, with the contribution needed to*

102

furnish each for the building.

10. Don't neglect raffles and sweepstakes.

The old-fashioned raffle was out of style for some time. Now, sophisticated fund raisers realize it still works hard; people still love the chance to win something they might never buy for themselves.

New York's Metropolitan Opera has an annual raffle that grows every year. A recent one offered 3,333 prizes, from traditionally desirable items such as cars, jewels and furs to the more offbeat—a tin of fresh caviar or a complete Italian wine cellar.

Important note: it pays to visualize raffle items in a simple leaflet and print the cash value of each.

A device used effectively by the private sector, but often overlooked by fund raisers, is the sweepstakes. One hospital for many years ran a national sweepstakes with $50,000 in cash prizes. According to postal regulations, no contribution was required of entrants, but one was suggested. A high percentage of those entering did give.

11. Make it easy to respond.

The easier you make it for the contributor to reply, the greater your response will be. It pays to enclose an envelope. However, return postage paid by the sender (which costs nothing unless activated) works just as well as a stamped envelope does.

Another helfpul insert is a card with the respondent's name and address, and a box to check amount of contribution. All the giver need do is write the check.

12. Create a sense of urgency.

Nothing lulls the senses more than the phrase "at your earliest convenience." *The Readers Digest* understands the value of urging prompt action. Most of their mailings make offers good only until a certain date. Set cut-off dates for matching-fund contributions. Offer bonus prizes for gifts received under a deadline.

MIT sent letters to delinquent previous givers just before graduation with an airmail envelope enclosed. The urgent appeal got results.

13. Acknowledge gifts promptly.

Politeness suggests immediate acknowledgment to contributors. Good fund-raising techniques demand it. The more personal you can make your thank you, the better. Can you have a secretary add a handwritten "Thank you very much" to the formal note?

14. Giving can be fun.

The business of fund raising does not have to be deadly serious. Letters and brochures written with warmth, charm and even relevant humor are more persuasive than chilly prose.

For successful fund raising, heed the advice of Benjamin Franklin: "Apply to all those whom you know will give something; next, to those whom you are uncertain whether they will give anything or not; and show them the list of those who have given; and lastly, do not neglect those you are sure will give nothing; for in some of them you will be mistaken.

Photography shot on location can add drama, when the location is relevant to the product.

CHAPTER XI

Catalogs
That Sell More

"We must let the goods speak for themselves," said Richard Warren Sears in 1897. Today, the Sears catalog does just that. Every one of the some 70,000 items have merchandise descriptions specifically written to emphasize the important facts customers should know before they buy. Instead of "selling the sizzle, not the steak," Sears does just the opposite.

The drapery section, for example, specifies information such as the weight and thread count of the fabric, the depths of hems, the type of hooks recommended for hanging. Even for fashion, still sold primarily on the styling, facts about the fabric, detailing and care are provided.

Sears believes the need for product information is greater than ever before. Of their nearly four billion dollars in annual catalog sales, 60 percent comes in by phone; and this part of the business is growing every day. Given all the facts, consumers will be able to buy more wisely and more economically.

Catalog shopping in general is seeing a revolution. The majority of purchasers are no longer rural, lower-income, less educated. Today's busy customers (especially working women) like the speed and convenience of buying from a book. Of course, the look and style that work for one type of product may not work for another. The lavish Gucci catalog, for instance, is chiefly devoted to full-page photographs, with no copy except brief descriptions found in the separate price list. The L. L. Bean catalog, on the other hand, uses three or four smaller photos to a page, with long descriptive copy. Both are hugely successful pieces; both appeal to very different audiences.

Establish Your Personality

The catalog must be an extension of the personality already communicated by your store or your product. Bloomingdale's image is one of contemporary chic; Cable Car Clothiers of San Francisco one of traditional English elegance.

Harrington's, which specializes in Vermont food products, makes every aspect of the catalog contribute to its personality of old-fashioned goodness. Covers feature Vermont scenes; photographs inside are deliberately black and white. Harrington's has retained the same personality in its catalogs for seventeen years, during which its list has grown from a handful of customers to more than 120,000.

Guidelines for Catalogs That Sell More Product

1. Use the cover to your best advantage.

Some catalogs start selling right on the

cover. Others use this space to build an image. Choose the cover treatment best for your product. Remember, the cover is your salesman's greeting at the half-opened door. It must work hard, in a short period of time, or the door will close.

> *Pfaelzer Brothers, marketers of gourmet meat products, produced an award-winning catalog which shows an old-fashioned butcher shop on the cover. Hanging sausages, sawdust on the floor, the butcher with his cleaver—all suggested the quality of the meat to be found on the pages inside. Successful results have led Pfaelzer's to mail envelopes with glassine windows or to send the catalog as a self-mailer, so customers see the cover immediately.*

2. The photographs should reflect the image.

"Catalogs are a visual medium," believes Jo-Von Tucker, who has created award winners for dozens of clients, including Neiman-Marcus and Horchow's. "The pictures must draw the customer to your merchandise. Make your photographs part of the unique design of your catalog— the reflection of your marketing image."

3. Use photographs instead of drawings.

It stands to reason that the more realistically you show the product, the better your catalog. Illustrate as many products as space allows. Usually, four-color photography works harder than black-and-white.

4. Pack the copy with facts, not fantasy.

The trick, say professional catalog writers, is to *anticipate* the customer's questions and answer them in the copy. The more you tell, the more you sell, especially when the product is an expensive one, or one that involves the consumer's well-being.

> *"The people who are going backpacking, for instance, depend on our products for their comfort," says a spokesman for Eddie Bauer, sellers of outdoor clothing and equipment. "They are vitally interested in details about zippers, buttons, reinforced bindings, weatherproofing, wind resistance, performance. We know from experience these customers read every word."*

5. Location shooting adds entertainment.

Photographic sessions outside the store add a note of visual excitement, as well as allowing you to take advantage of natural lighting that cannot be simulated inside the studio. Locations can be as simple as the park across the street, or as complex as a trip around the world. Note that use of locations is most effective when it is *relevant* to the products.

> *Neiman-Marcus presented its annual fur collection in a catalog photographed on a cruise that visited Scandinavia, Russia and the North Cape. Models in Russian sable in front of the Winter Palace in Leningrad were a natural.*

*Bloomingdale's saluted the beginning of the
store's extensive new import program by
photographing the catalog almost entirely in
Mainland China.*

6. Change pace now and then.

Have the courage to devote a full-page
feature, or even a two-page spread, to unique
items. (This is a technique pioneered by
Horchow's.) The visual surprise calls attention to
the merchandise and also serves as a refreshing
change in layout.

7. Select appropriate models.

Models must be chosen so they relate to the
items being sold and to the target audience. Your
customer should want to look like the people in
the photographs.

*Cutter Bill, Texas stores dealing in Western
specialties, needed models who looked
comfortable in jeans and boots, and could
ride horses.*

8. Don't waste space.

Every inch in your catalog is precious; make
each contribute to the sale. For some products,
the most efficient use of space is luxurious two-
page spreads; for others, a "busy" look with many
products displayed adds to sales.

*L. L. Bean, which has been mailing its
catalog for over sixty years, believes in
using every page to display the maximum
number of products. A recent sixty-four-*

page piece pictured 243 different items.

9. Make it easy to order.

Every device that makes it more convenient for the customer adds to the chance you will make a sale. A bound-in order blank helps. So does a postage-paid envelope. A good order blank allows the customer ample space to write in necessary information, such as number of items, and, if you accept credit cards, the card number. Remind the customer in subheads to fill out the form completely: "Remember to include size and color."

> *Catalogs have a long life. If you are binding in an order form, always include complete order information separately within the catalog as well. Prospects will read it long after the form has been torn out.*

10. Consider special catalogs for special markets.

Draw attention to a new line of products with a separate mini-catalog. Or design a catalog for a particular target audience (travelers, wine lovers, children).

> *The Metropolitan Museum of Art saluted the opening of its new Children's Bookshop with a catalog devoted to presents for the young. It features a Sumerian race game, a punch-out medieval town, Colonial dolls and, of course, a stuffed replica of "William," the Museum's hippopotamus mascot.*

11. Repeat your winners.

Those tried-and-true products that always garner orders should be the flagships of your catalog. Give them prominence in the most important spots: the first eight pages, the last eight, and, if you bind in an order form, the pages around it. Give new items good position so you can evaluate how well they perform.

Establish a level of performance, and weed out products that fail to meet it.

12. Mail to your list often.

The professionals say it pays to mail four, five, six times a year—and more. Mail even more often to your best customers; they are also your best *prospects*. Keep trolling for new names. Consider a smaller, less expensive version of your basic catalog as a lure for these new purchasers.

13. Why not charge for your catalog?

Indications are that a consumer may consider a catalog of more value if it costs something. While most catalogs are still free, the trend is increasingly to a nominal charge of one to two dollars.

> *The Gucci catalog is the Rolls Royce of the business, at a cost of eight dollars.*
> *However, it contains a gift certificate of eight dollars which can be applied to any purchase of fifty dollars or more.*

14. Include a personalized letter.

A letter to the customer—particularly a new prospect—increases chances of a sale as much as

25 percent. Make the letter as personal as you can. One way to personalize and urge the consumer to take action is by affixing a name-and-address label to the mailing. The buyer simply peels the label off and pastes it onto the order form. Simple, but effective.

15. Consider telephone marketing.

If your average order is now over twenty-five dollars, investigate orders by telephone, whether you run it yourself or hire a marketing service. Professional telephone marketers, while expensive, tend to pay for themselves in the short run. Purchasing by phone is the wave of the future. It pays to check it out.

> *The average telephone order is a larger amount of money than the average mail order. Big-ticket items sell better over the phone than less expensive ones. And a two-way conversation gives you the chance to sell additional items to the same customer.*

16. Test! And test some more!

The secret to successful mail-order selling lies in endless testing. Check out every aspect of the mailing: envelope, cover, the kind of merchandise displayed, sale or premium offers, bonus gifts for fast action, everything.

> *Sears and Montgomery Ward use more than 170 different cells to determine to whom to send special catalogs and fliers.*

The catalog is your salesman in the home. *It must represent you at your best, tell the truth, instill confidence in the customer and, above all, create a desire to purchase.*

The place to start selling is right on the envelope—or risk being thrown away.

CHAPTER XII

More Successful Direct Marketing

Direct marketing is any type of marketing which asks for a *response* from the prospect. It includes direct mail, telephone, space advertising, catalogs and *any* advertising where a coupon, telephone number or other response device is used. This marketing also embraces the newer "electronic" response devices that are now changing the face of the industry.

The future is bright. Direct marketing caters to in-home, at-leisure response and purchase in an era when more people have more time on their hands. For direct mail alone, the Gallup Organization estimates that each day 29 million consumers receive a mailed request. One of their studies showed that four out of ten had purchased something in the previous six months as the result of a mailing.

Creativity Is the Key to Better Response

Many experts worry that direct marketing these days is being done too much by rote. "Direct marketers are playing it 'too safe,' going for small gains with little risk instead of the big breakthrough," says Caroline Zimmermann, President of Zimmermann Marketing, Inc. "But in fact the right creative message is just as important as the right list or the right offer."

Like any other advertising medium, direct response works better when you decide on a strategy and other important issues in advance.

- Promise the prospect something meaningful. Your offer will fail unless it contains a benefit. Appeal to basic human needs: desire to make more money, to be more attractive.
- Understand your target audience. Speak their language (and never speak down to them). Understand not only their demographics (their income, for instance) but their psychographics (how they spend their income).
- Don't be afraid of long copy. The more you tell, the more you sell, especially when you are marketing big-ticket items, such as cars or vacations.
- It pays to be specific rather than general. If readers are interested enough to read on, they are hungry for facts.
- Choose a format appropriate to the audience—and the product. A mailing from a savings bank appealing to prospects nearing retirement age should look very different from a record offer to teenagers.

Set Goals and Test Response

"The most successful people in direct marketing are people who thrive on being measured," says direct-response great Robert Stone. Test every element of the total package—copy, layout, lists, premium, sweepstakes, pricing. Establish in advance what results will constitute success or failure. For example, magazines must often wait for *renewal* results before they can truly evaluate an offer.

Don't just judge amount of response itself. Also take into account *cost per inquiry,* and *conversion rate* from inquiry to sale.

Innovate

Once upon a time, the sweepstakes was a new idea. So was the Yes/No token. What are the breakthrough response ideas of the next decade?

Invite new talent to lend their brains to problem solving. Don't be afraid to be creative. Understand you will have to spend money to test new products and ideas.

Fifteen Direct Response Ideas

1. Capitalize on the "Hot Spots."

Some areas of mailing are more important than others—envelope, front panel of a brochure, reply card and P.S. Make these important areas work hard for you. The P.S., especially, should be used to restate or reinforce a copy point.

Handwritten marginal notes add impact, if they are not overused. They can draw the reader's attention to an important copy point, or add a note of urgency or news.

2. Flag the prospect on the envelope.

This is the first place to get impact and start your sale.

The Paul Taylor Dance Group used a perforated envelope with copy that referred to two separate letters inside. It said: "Read this letter if you love Paul Taylor and are a fan of modern dance."

And: "Read this letter if you've never seen Paul Taylor and have serious doubts about modern dance."

The mailing was extremely successful. It flagged not only its primary target audience of modern dance fans, but a broader secondary audience as well.

3. Consider special envelope devices.

Simulation of a handwritten return address is effective, especially if you are using a celebrity and can suggest the letter is coming directly from him or her. A recent test that used a celebrity's name and address boosted response by more than 20 percent.

A bright, boldly colored envelope can have enormous impact. And, surprisingly, it works very well for upscale products, too. If you are mailing a colorful brochure, consider an envelope with a clear window to let the color show through.

Another effective device is informing the reader there is a free gift or money-saving offer inside.

4. Try for a memorable address.

It pays to have an address or box number people can remember, especially for direct-response advertising on television or radio.

The British Travel Association prodded

memories by using the historic date of the Norman Conquest, 1066, as its P.O. box number.

Consult your post office.

5. Be personal, be human.

Personalize more than the salutation. One credit card company increased its membership by including a personalized order form for the credit card, already made out with the prospect's name.

Don't be afraid to be human. Too much direct mail sounds as if it were written by a computer.

McArthur's Smoke House uses whimsy with good effect. They end their letter with the suggestion that the respondent fill in the order form and "fold any old way to fit into an old envelope."

6. Don't forget "Free," "Now" and other magic words.

The old standbys still have power. Use "half price," "last chance," "limited time only," "bargain," "sale" and other tried-and-true persuaders. They work!

7. Involve the reader.

Give the reader something to do: a Yes/No token to paste on the reply card, a blank to scratch that reveals whether he has won or lost. Make the involvement device relevant to the product.

"Is your dream career in the stars? Find out

with this do-it-yourself astrology quiz."
That's how one magazine involved
prospective subscribers on the envelope of a
mailing which contained reprints of a recent
article. This involving device allowed
readers to sample the editorial style of the
magazine.

8. Ask the reader to take action.

Never let the prospect off the hook. Dramatize reject offers, for instance. "Release the free casserole you have set aside in my name and make it available to someone else."

Use a deadline to add urgency and overcome human inertia. It pays to offer a bonus for quick action (perhaps with a decreasing bonus for those who act later).

Another way to get involvement is by
converting the prospect from a passive
accepter to an active "order placer." Betty
Crocker does this successfully with the offer
of a free recipe cardbox. The prospect must
select the color—a psychological step
forward.

9. Dramatize savings.

Don't say "You save thirty-nine cents." Make it quickly apparent this is real money with a coupon or check also enclosed.

House and Garden magazine enclosed a
check for $6.03 good on a one-year
subscription. Prospects were asked to mail
it back endorsed.

Always establish the value of a gift or premium. One company did this for a free pen it offered by including the pen, at its regular price, in the catalog sent in the same mailing.

10. Consider premiums and prizes relevant to the product.

You can raise the quality of people responding if the prize or premium relates to the product or service.

> *The Garden Way Company (a maker of garden equipment) offered a roto tiller as the grand prize in a sweepstakes. Those who entered the contest were prime prospects for a salesman's call.*

Don't exclude more general premiums, however, without careful testing.

11. Premiums don't have to be expensive.

A thirty-five-cent cookbook increased response 17 percent over a chafing dish that cost ten times more. And the company ended up with its own exclusive premium.

Be innovative in the premiums you offer. (Always test new ideas to be sure, however). And keep in mind the psychographics of the prospects you want to attract.

> *A sweepstakes appealing to an upscale target audience successfully offered framed autographs of famous people as prizes, with the grand prize a signature of Napoleon. This fresh approach appealed to the high-*

income, educated prospects. And the Napoleon signature cost less than the usual grand prize, a new car!

12. Consider mailing to your list more often.

It is an old direct-response motto that you should keep repeating your winners. Repeat mailings that are profitable to the same lists. The Franklin Mint mails fifty times a year! Resist changing for change's sake.

13. Explore new prospect sources other than mail.

As postal costs rise and lists are plumbed, you must be inventive in looking at new sources.

Upscale magazines might find new prospects by placing copies of the publication, with special-rate subscription offers, in specially selected hotel rooms—only deluxe rooms and suites.

14. Use local media to support a mailing.

Advertise in local newspapers, radio and even television to alert prospects of your mailing. Don't forget to include an 800 number (or other response mechanism) in such advertising so that people who did not receive the mailing have a way of requesting it.

15. "Decoy" your own offers.

Fill in your own coupon, call your 800 number, mail back the faulty merchandise and ask for a refund. Chances are you will find something that can be improved.

A corollary of this rule is: check out the list

before you mail. Call ten names at random to make sure they really live there.

Future Trends

For some years, direct-marketing sages have predicted a revolution created by new communications methods. Yet traditional methods continue to dominate the industry. The impact of new forces such as electronic media, access mechanisms, and satellites is only beginning to be felt.

Cable TV has begun to experiment with access mechanisms where advertisers will pay only for actual inquiries. Some marketers are investigating hotel-room cable possibilities, which will permit the customer to peruse restaurant, entertainment and sightseeing possibilities in the city he is visiting.

Satellites may soon make international direct marketing feasible, and consumers will be able to call one 800 number to purchase a dress from Paris or a stereo from Tokyo.

Telephone marketing is the fastest moving of these newer methods. Approximately eight billion is done annually, and indications are that this volume will increase at least 10 percent within the next few years. Some tips for telephone marketing include:

• 800 numbers work more efficiently for higher-priced items. The New York State Department of Commerce successfully advertised weekend packages to New York City, at an average price of over $300 per couple.

• The average telephone order is 20 percent larger than write-in.

• Once you have a customer on the telephone, try to sell him something more. Suggest sales and "specials."

• Be sure to indicate in your mail or advertising exactly what hours the telephone number can be reached.

• Unless you have had a good deal of experience dealing with telephone marketing firms, it pays to work through brokers who can match your particular needs with companies who can fill them.

As competition grows fiercer, so does the importance of fresh creative approaches. Define your problem. Aim for innovative solutions. Then, test—always test—to make sure they will work.

About the Author

Jane Maas is the president of Muller Jordan Weiss Advertising. She is the first woman to become head of a major agency she did not found herself.

Mrs. Maas is perhaps best known for her direction of the "I Love New York" program—including its brochures. She is also co-author of the now classic How to Advertise (*St. Martin's, 1975*).

Acknowledgments

The author would like to thank the following individuals for generous contributions of time and expertise:

Robert Beyers, Stanford University, Stanford, Calif.
Joel J. Blattstein, Schein/Blattstein Advertising, New York, N.Y.
Bud Brettelle and Art Goldman, Chenault Associates, New York, N.Y.
Kenneth Brock and Treece de Santis, New York Hospital, New York, N.Y.
Suzan Couch, Warner Amex Communications, New York, N.Y.
Joan Capelin, Haines, Lundberg, Waehler, New York, N.Y.
Jane Cohn, Dudley, Anderson, Yutzy, New York, N.Y.
Gary Frank, Gardner, Stein & Frank, Chicago, Ill.
Burr Gibson, Marts and Lundy, New York, N.Y.
Milton Glaser, Milton Glaser, Inc., New York, N.Y.
Donald Kersting, Kersting & Brown, New York, N.Y.
James Kobs, Kobs and Brady Advertising, Chicago, Ill.
Natel Matschulat, New York State Department of Commerce, New York, N.Y.
Mrs. John A. Morris, Girl Scout Council of Greater New York, New York, N.Y.
Dennis O'Brien, Bucknell University, Lewisburg, Penna.
Neil Ostergren, Americana Hotels, New York, N.Y.
Anthony D. Paolini, Sears Roebuck, Chicago, Ill.
Kenneth Roman, Jr. and Al Nelson, Ogilvy and Mather, Inc., New York, N.Y.
Harold Singer, Wells, Rich, Greene, Inc., New York, N.Y.
Emily Soell, Rapp and Collins, New York, N.Y.
Norman Tissian, Spiro and Associates, Philadelphia, Penna.
Jo-Von Tucker, The Photographers Inc., Irving, Texas
Walter Weintz, Walter Weintz and Co., Stamford, Conn.
Mary Zahn, New York, N.Y.
Caroline Zimmermann, Zimmermann Marketing, Inc., New York, N.Y.

And to seven very special people who encouraged me to persevere on this project. At Wells, Rich, Greene, Inc.: Mary Wells Lawrence, Charlie Fredericks, Marty Stern and Dolores Zahn. And at home, Jenny, Kate and Michael Maas.